Sometimes You Gotta Let The Pain Out

Lateasha Owens

BookLeaf Publishing

India | USA | UK

Presentation by *BookLeaf Publishing*

Web: www.bookleafpub.com

E-mail: info@bookleafpub.com

ISBN:9789360944643

First edition 2024

DEDICATION

To my "Daddy," my beloved father, Louis "Avon" Owens, whose nightly bedtime stories not only nurtured my love for books and writing, but also cultivated a boundless curiosity within me.

To my bonus mom, my "T Lady," Joan Owens, a constant beacon of unwavering belief in my dreams and creative pursuits.

Thank you both for your unconditional love that has been a source of strength, shaping my understanding of compassion and resilience. Even during your physical absence, I can still feel the two of you near. Protecting me as if you were still here.

With heartfelt gratitude and boundless love,

Snuk

ACKNOWLEDGEMENT

I extend my heartfelt gratitude to my sister, Avonette Blanding, for being a constant well of knowledge, source of encouragement and always pushing me toward greatness. Your continued support for my artsy fartsy endeavors will never go unnoticed.
I love you endlessly.

To my muse, ladybug,
What's sweeter than a honeybun?
Thank you for selflessly supporting me throughout my journey back to self.

To the pain endured and those who inflicted it:
They say focus shifts when pain is involved. Well, look now—I have FINALLYreleased my book! Thanks for being the unexpected inspiration.

I love you, and I forgive you.
Xoxo

PREFACE

This collection of poems is my way of finally releasing what was never mine to begin with. A narration of repetitive cycles, rooted in generations of painful experiences that I never realized I didn't deserve to hold so tightly.

Sometimes you gotta resurrect the pain that's been buried deep within. Extracting it from every crevice and every ancestral wound that's bled onto the fabric of your existence, genetically buried within your cells, or projected onto one's soul involuntarily.

Although our pain and experiences mold us into who we are. It is our duty to transcend, heal and rewrite the narrative. Over the years, ARTiculating pain through my art has assisted me with processing painful experiences, in navigating the healing process, in emotionally unpacking, coping and managing anger. I've allowed pain to live rent free in the pages of my diaries all my life. In my music. In my art. In my poems. But I now realize, even with all the multifaceted forms of artistic expression. I never fully let the pain OUT. I've hoarded all the deep painful writings, fearing judgment, shame, disownment and further abandonment. I've clung on to this pain, wielding it like a sacred shield blanketing the darkness. Turns out it was my own shame silencing my truth.

This book is my way of courageously letting the light in and the pain out. It's time to bury this pain somewhere else. I am not a coffin, but a vessel for transformation. I am allowing this darkness to be illuminated, devoured, by building brighter connections. May these pages not only echo my journey, but serve as a beacon of light for those who may feel trapped in darkness. A reminder that they are not alone in their struggles; the light is always deep within. I've lost A LOT throughout my journey; but thankfully I've never lost HOPE. I never lost my light.

 One of the most powerful things I've learned is to forgive myself for the pain I've projected, as well as for what I've allowed myself to endure while being wounded and operating in survival mode. Learning to love that unhealed side of myself that didn't know any better. Composing this book helped me realize, I am not that person anymore and I deserve to give myself more grace. Over the years, my poetry has truly evolved, and so have I.

Table of Contents

Fumble

My story is so complex
I don't know where to begin.
If it's where Tea stopped…
SYKO popped, and SPAZ ascends
All I know is that it needs to be told
It's a must that I destroy this mold,
unfold and fly… soar
I'm like a once tamed lion
Now in preparation to roar
Seeking out my platform and perfect time
With eloquent wording…
But then I realized that "perfection" is improper
verbing, for my plight..
Yeah I know "verbing" isn't a word... but it's
alright.
KEEP sight…

Focus on my point.
I'm attempting to shed my social conditioning…
Repositioning, for greatness.
No longer being concerned with this SAFE life
bizz…
More so trying to LIVE.
Prosper.
Shutting off my mental TV and gossip,
about irrelevant shit…
So again.
I don't know WHERE to begin.
I just know I'm ready…
Embracing my fear cause it's part of me… and I
have to acknowledge it in order to release.
Knowing that I have to increase my confidence
Know my capabilities and walk in them
Encourage others through my story.
Teach lessons through my struggle.
Stop being afraid,
then regret letting myself fumble.

Things I Never Said

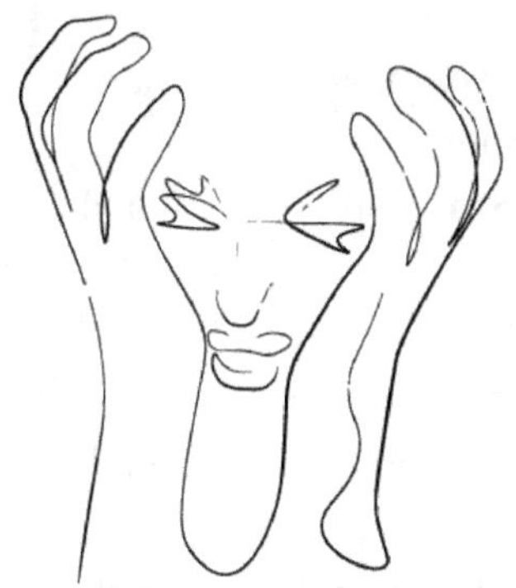

What I never said is "I'm scared to death"
But not ready to die.
Wishing I was fearless
But for some reason skeptical
Pondering the outcome of "a try"
What I never said was "I'm not sure if my
decision to never take meds is right… or if being
stubborn and holistic minded will ruin my life."
I never said I sporadically hallucinate and
mentally skip time.
I never once mentioned how sorry I was for
stressing my family out
Knowing this fight ain't only mine.
Did I care?
Mmm, yeah… but, hell…
This is my life, my mind, MY brain; they said
"dying."
My pain, my loss, my dreams, my sky.

Black!!!

Sometimes not knowing how to act,
I decided not to.
I decided to take off the mask and be vulnerable.

Why hide??

Fukk you and your opinions, fukk getting in my
feelings…
fukk YOU if you think I'm playing victim!!

FuCK the government,
Columbus, and the sail they SAID shipped 'em!!

Clearly THEY say a lot…
America ain't right… and won't be till we're
fixed.

They're playing with our food, hearts and minds
now we're PHYSICALLY sick!!
With shit once never heard of—made up
patented illnesses.

Call it modern warfare.
Commercialized crime…
We're killing our cells,
while corporations live off of OUR dime!!

Manipulating OUR TRUTH,
corrupting OUR youth
Selling OUR hair!
and OUR share is nowhere!

But I never said this…

I don't wanna die like this!

Not before embracing the chance to help heal
my people; enlighten a few sheeple.

Before becoming disciplined and healing
myself—making peace with the cards I've been
dealt.

Before detaching from fears and learning to live
FREELY!!

Before sharing my gifts with the world
completely.

Before seeing my siblings conquer their demons.

NOT BEFORE conquering MS, giving my
family hope—something to believe in.

Misunderstood

While you were out standing in Jordan lines
They were signing dotted lines
Plotting on our demise
Laughing at our failure to realize we're being
HAD
Black bodies lying in streets, while we sit back
and tweet, 'bout how we knew 'em
How he stayed fresh and "had all the bitches."
Yet his main chick couldn't carry out his dying
wishes; to "bury me a G"
He never had a life insurance policy.
But "had every pair of Dopes."

Made stacks selling coke…
However, when that blood flooded his air
passages, he choked.
Nothing heroic about being savagely slain…

Why not leave a positive legacy behind your
name?
Be the ONE who got away, who attempted to
empower millions, and uplift the hood
Teach our youth that failure is not an option, just
cause you're misunderstood.

Pieces Of My Mind

When you're from the hood
Your entire existence is claimed to be
misunderstood.
But they knew.

The conditions they made for us, only make us
stronger
resilient,
brilliant even.
But we don't even see it,
too busy thieving.

Trying to steal empty identities, of those who'd
prefer to look like WE.
Who pay TOP dollar to have curves like she,
and length like he…
then decompose before the cradle
cause they aren't melanated like WE.

WE'RE STRONG Y'ALL!!

Embrace your beauty.
Adjust your crown!
Take notice, we're the only "race" STILL
STANDING,
who's CONTINUOUSLY knocked down!!
FROWNED upon, hated!
Purposely miseducated!

Hidden secrets of greatness CAN'T be
suppressed forever.

Let's take the initiative to rise up, TOGETHER!

We been been,
storming through this weather.
We been been,
surviving in these streets.
When will we CHOOSE to reposition the heat!!?
Readjust the target…
reevaluate the market!

Our culture ain't for sale.
Our men aren't BIRTHED for jail,
free labor, and the characteristics of sheep.

They're birthed to obtain knowledge,
reclaim power

and build up where they sleep!

Instead, they're out here claiming streets.
Staying "strapped with the heat"
Taking lives over irrelevant shit!
Having "fukk niggaz" houses hit.

Whole time, you ah fuk nigga yourself!!
Placing life beneath wealth.

Thinking that karma won't circle back…

My negus, we gotta be knowledgeable bout
MORE than a "well organized" trap!

Stop being MENTALLY trapped!!!!

It's time we wake up and clap BACK,
on MORE than social media!

Kids dying in these streets,
black images being slaughtered and slandered,
IN THE MEDIA!

Then dummies going out and imitating what
they see on te-LIE-vision.

How bout you emanate peace and promote
UNITY, instead of division?!

Set standards, and change the game!!

Love YOURSELVES AND DEMAND
RESPECT from your oppressors!!
Stop assuming you're the shit,
just cause it's Polo cologne and knock off
Chanel on your dresser.
Cause you copped an extended clip,
and walkn' around with an imaginary vest on.

Karma comes back!!

To you,
your kids…
your immediate fam and friends.

Don't think you're untouchable!
Don't THINK your so called "loyal bitch" ain't
fuckable!!!

Get your mind on the NOW!!
Negus walking 'round possessing unused
crowns,
and powers from ancestors.

Wasting REAL talent on shit like sports and
wack rappin'

trappn' and ass clappn... complaints with NO
action!!

..and we wondering what happened to our
youth??!
Y'all ain't ready for the truth!!
Cause the truth is,
you did… YOU did…
and so did I!!
So busy focused on "MY."

My this, and my that…

Yet her mama's on crack, and his daddy's locked
up…
and now he and she fucked!!

...and he and she only 15..

Babies raising babies;
cause now baby's one and she's sixteen!

...and she was never raised herself!

Now HE's gone,
cause he's playing out the cards he was dealt.

His momma never had no help!
He's thinking, "why I gotta help her?"

His pops was a "street nigga," and "had hella
Louie V belts…"
All the "hood niggas respected him," he hit the
block,
They FLOCKED to his car!
Yet neglected to tell him,
"Go home and raise your son,
…he coppn' drinks out the bar."

"He might be fukkn too…"
All cause he's trying to fill the void of NOT
feeling loved by you.
NOW he's pumping babies into her…
Immature minds easily blur, without proper
guidance and knowledge.

Instead of giving them what they want, give
them what they NEED!
These kids aren't all bad, we're just neglecting to
properly LEAD…
and our problems aren't ALL the white man's
fault,
at this point they're OURS!
For eons we've BELIEVED the lie that we have
no power.

We DO!!

The power resides in our numbers.

ME, plus you!!
Our melanated brains,
Our OX like strength
and our untapped gifts!

So remove the fog and seize the day!!
Our ancestors left behind NOTES in our DNA!!!

Obedient Conditioning

We must stop measuring our strength by the
amount of pain we're able to endure.

Our ancestors strength was measured in how
fearlessly they overcame adversities.

How they refused to be physically, mentally and
spiritually enslaved by their oppressors.

Now we're willing to hand over power… for
F-R-E-E!!
QUEEN, you ain't free!!
Ass shots, tummy tucks and veneers,
Sometimes over already perfect teeth…

Sounds like inflation on mental slavery to me…
and we're cool with paying the fee!!

Then we hop on social media and gas each other,
like "yesss bitch!! Lemme see!!?"

Why TF aren't we EMPOWERED!!??
Why TF aren't we enraged!!!??

They're manipulating our ignorance,
our socially engineered self hate…

Got us thinking the best body gon' get us the
validation and acceptance we've always craved.
The life partner of our dreams, that'll think twice
before calling another bitch bae.

My negus we ain't FREE,
I call that mentally enslaved!!

We constantly misbehave.
Then expect our kids to get it right.
Meanwhile proper guidance is out of sight.

We sit on social media every day and all night.

Microdosing validation
Further aligning with their agenda of self-hatred
Comparing our cells to mfs living a facade
To people who mask their reality w/ expensive
trips and Pretty Little Things...
Filters to cover up every time it rains.

What happened to authenticity??
Maybe if we lived more REALISTICALLY, our
younger generation could use it as a blueprint to
know that life isn't ALWAYS laced with crystal
stairs.

But when you develop the courage to face your
inner demons—embrace your flaws, have fun,
but work hard.
You'll break the cycle.

It won't be cute when they grow up and make
the same mistakes like you..

The world has already stacked billion dollar
distractions on our path.
Poisoned our food, to intentionally disrupt our
MOODS…
autoimmune this, immunocompromised that.

When will we become fed the fuck up, UNITE
and take our muthafukkn power back?!!??

Call it cognitive dissonance.
Call it united in resistance.

Just don't call it obedient conditioning.

Solitude

Out of nearly 4yrs of trying to prove my love,
my loyalty,

What I'm most proud of…
I never tried to prove my value
for those who didn't see it

Sucks for them.

I spent so much time trying to prove things to
people from whom I received bare minimum
and mediocracy in return.

Surface level love.
That "I'm too scared to be hurt again, so I'll only
give a PIECE of my heart" type love.

I was never perfect.
But, when I loved, I LOVED!
With my WHOLE heart.
Only to receive scraps in return.
I fought to prove my loyalty.

In my solitude,
I realized I only betrayed myself.
Bloody knuckles.
Popped stitches.
From wounds that I thought mended.

I've loved
and I've lost...but thankfully, I NEVER lost me.

I was always able to find ME.

My light is one of my most valuable assets.
It leads me out of ANY darkness, and back to
source.
Back to my core self.

It's crazy how people circle back checkn' for
you, when you're numb.

When you've decided that you're done.

When you make your way through the pain and
realize, YOU'RE the prize

and that you've won!

In my solitude I realized that I've come across
some romantic mf's!!

They knew me well
Knew exactly how to woo me, then disappeared
whenever I fell.

My toxic trait?

I never FELL out of love.
OUT of being wooed.

In my solitude,
I've realized,
materialistic shit was always poured into me…
People always bought their way back into my
heart
and I allowed it…
Never again.

I forgive myself for not knowing I was,
PRICELESS!!
So correction,
I THOUGHT I knew my value.
Whole time, I depreciated while loving you.

I minimized my standards.

I allowed myself to be bought.
In my solitude, I realized no one took advantage
of their access.
Over time, they'd become inconsistent.
Resentful. Passive. Dismissive.

In my solitude,
I realized people struggled to love me,
PROPERLY.
They loved the idea of infinity WITH me;
until I revealed my complexities.
My boundaries.

In my solitude,
I realized that some of my boundaries were
beautifully engineered by insecurities.

But back to my point.

I realized my complexities were intimidating to
some,
maybe most.

I had morals and standards..
and the double Cap—Gemini Moon in me kept
me assertive with both!!
Even at times when my OWN shit wasn't
together,
I still let it be known!!

"Don't fuk wit' me!!"
I'll be ghost!!

In my solitude,
I've realized that unpacking is a very intricate
part of this healing game.
You can't suppress.
You can't finesse your way out of the work.
Cause YOU is what will always be staring back.

That mirror NEVER misses a blemish
and best believe if you falter,
karma gon' have your sentence.

In my solitude,
I realized that throughout my life,
people often loved me with their wallets and
verbs.
Resulting in me being left feeling unheard.
Unloved… and gas lit with lies.
Unkept promises lead to my demise.

From a child, I reached for love.
I seeked LOVE.
But like the word "seeked" in the dictionary,
it was never found…

EYE was the protector.
The healer.

The forgiver.
But I don't know if I ever LIVED

In my solitude.
I've learned to prioritize ME.
I LEARNED to pour into ME!!!
After YEARS of pouring into empty cups that
rarely poured back...
and when they DID,
It was nutrients that lacked.
Or immediately they'd deplete me, by needing
what they poured, BACK.

But I forgive myself.
Even forgave them.

Had to forgive myself for not acknowledging the
manipulation.
For allowing the strangulation…
I constantly gasped for air, yet nothing was
there.

Nature relit my flame whenever I'd lose my
spark.
Over the years, I've grown numb…
normalized being loved improperly.
Even found toxic ways to reciprocate love, with
beautiful verbs…

Sometimes having no intentions of backing my
words. But I matured.

In my solitude, it was my inner child this time
that I found and adored.
She reminded me of that old saying—
"hurt people, hurt people."

That it's never personal.
Also, that forgiveness doesn't always mean
regained access.

Maybe I never became a biological parent
because I had to re-parent ME.
In my solitude,
eye seen ME!

Firstly, I'm dope and magical AF!!
I trust that source will one day send a lover that
values my depth;
that isn't threatened once they see the rarity of
my soul.

Someone who reminds me of it, during moments
I forget, as I grow old.

A partner I can dive intellectually deep with…
make love in the oceans of their mind;
no life jackets, no judgment.

Everyone has their limits.
But why??
Maybe they're afraid of what they'd find.

In my solitude,
I learned I desire genuine connections.
Emotional depth and maturity.
A partner who values quality time over
distractions.
Someone who's down to do the work,
You'll rarely catch them slackn'.

Someone who's not intimidated by my light.
Someone who acknowledges true love,
and surrenders to the urge of fight or flight.

Janè sè qua

Feminine energy is magnetic, prophetic even…
See I'm different,
I'll take a semi-soft womban over a queen still
fully operating in her masculine season.
I don't want your unchecked ego,
I became too acquainted with healing my lover's
pain
I'd began to think love wasn't worth having
unless it came with darkness I had to help chase
away.
At a point, my healing spirit became entangled
in my own ego.
I didn't know I was infatuated w/ chasing love
I didn't KNOW my abandonment issues taught
me that fighting to be seen was a normal phase
of love.

I didn't KNOW what emotional manipulation
was
I had no fucking clue that emotional abuse was
worse than physical...
I was grown AF, learning that emotional
cheating could be worse than a mf being
intimately into you!!

So yea, I'll take a semi-soft womban over a
queen still operating in her masculine energy,
any day.
Cause them semi-soft women are LEARNING.
They're actively DOING the work.
They've at LEAST discovered there's a soft side
that exists, and they're allowing that side of
themselves to come out and play.

They're learning they no longer need their egos
and curves to get their way.

They're learning that they no longer have to
mentally manipulate to get their needs met...

They're learning that their natural beauty is
beyond heaven sent.

They're embracing their authenticity.
They're okay with not being perfect.
Finding perfection in their imperfections.

Releasing self judgment.
Stepping outside of comfort zones and providing
THEMSELVES w/ validation

Yea, that's my type of Queen
More like a Ghetto Goddess!!
I like that title better, it kinda has a ring…

A certain janè sè qua

This is me kissing my attraction to toxic women
goodbye!!

Alignment

Let me…

Fuck ya Chakras into alignment!

Caress your spine with these,
predicates and verbs of mine

Allow our souls to intertwine

Fill you with a piece, of mine

Fly you on my spaceship pass mars

Jupiter.

Maybe Saturn too…

Cause your mental beauty is beyond this world,
and I haven't even spoken to you…

Yet.

However,
I've already tapped into your mindset,
and invaded your thoughts.

Your entire existence is viscous!
...and similar to a prey I am CAUGHT!

UP,
in your galactic energy…

I'm diggin' you…
you feelin' me?

Now back to these chakras…

Let my words seduce your molecular structure…

Align your atoms in a linear fashion.

Send vibrations through your body and every
vertebrae of your thoracic.
I can already see your heart chakra dancing…

Although your third eye and crown chakra are
what I seek.

Your sacral area is calling meee...

And I'm listenin',
paying attention.

Over standing.

Your root is demanding.

Let's connect.. .

Eye see you.

Eye imagine your aura is magic

I imagine your sex groans to be as captivating as
melodic moans

Similar to, and as nurturing, as isochronic
tones…

Stimulating to my brain
amongst other parts unknown.

I got so caught up in writing this for you,
I almost felt like I wrote it for self too.

Cause I love me so much that,
loving you reminded me of how my self-love
felt...

I guess aligning you, aligned us

Now I'm baffled…

But,

trust…

Me,
when eye say…
it was led to happen this way.

Your solar plexus is open and filled with
abundant light…

Asé

Sometimes You Gotta Check Yourself

I was where I was supposed to be,
until I wasn't.

Growing uncontrollably free

Abundant
like weeds…
Searching for a purpose,
a way to be of service

without sucking the life out of anything,
or anyone.

Healthy connections only.
Looking to add to…

Pondering on life.
Love.
Peace, non toxic connections…
intimacy without attachment,
to any specific narrative.
Fluidly creating magic...
Growing.
Building.

Openly receiving,
without questioning what's being given.

I search for reasons to love harder...
To usher in strength, confidence and wisdom.
To be present in my Queendom
My temple needs me most...

Fearing abandonment,
meanwhile ghosting CELL'f

Voluntarily giving away power
putting self healing on shelf.

Preoccupied…
chasing so called lovers and monetary wealth.
Failing to realize,
All I need is within cell'f.

Chokehold

I tend to runaway from myself
Not quite sure how to stay
Abandonment was all I've ever known
Not quite sure how to play; keeps.

Longest term love was a fable
Unable to connect emotionally
Trauma bond morphed into something unstable.

Eye never knew I was being emotionally abused
Gas lit…

Being emotionally cheated on was new
So, I accepted it.
Normalized it.
Labeled it, the "best love I'd ever had…"

Even my therapist at the time said "don't leave,
your son's life will be misled… he needs you."

"Without you, what will he have?? A life full of
enablers, it'll definitely turn out bad."

Needless to say,
I later needed therapy, for my therapist.
A therapist, for what my initial therapist missed

He'd unfortunately led me astray
Later I developed the strength to walk away…

Right, into the arms… of another trauma bond.

Thought it was magic!!
Realized I allowed ole' girl to wreak havoc!

This time my nervous system was the target.
She loved me so hard with her wallet!!
I ain't NEVER allowed myself to be a bought
bitch!!
But I called myself surrendering to love… whole
time got quicksand in.

Anxiety had me in a chokehold
Cliffhanger, the end...
Not sure if I'm ready for this story to be told.

Dark Kiss
(channeling generational pain)

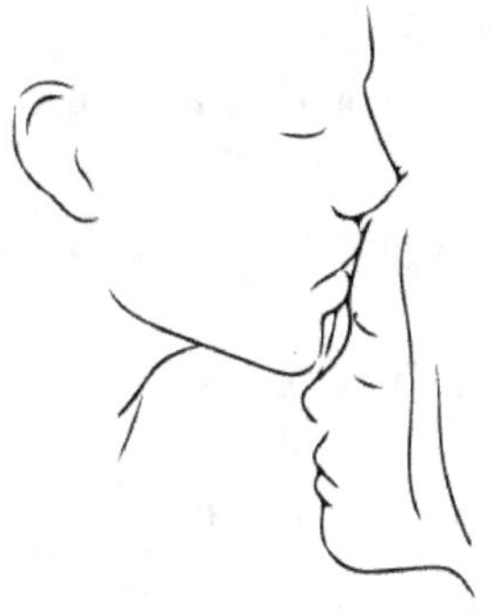

I wasn't old enough to know normal wasn't what
it was,
Until I was old enough to realize a life lived in
survival mode wasn't what it was,
supposed to be…
It was supposed to be love,
Emotions. Vulnerability.
Building memorable bonds with siblings.
Instead…we bonded over scars.
Comparing horror stories
betting on what'll be in store for tomorrow.
Who'll catch it first!!?

Can you imagine??
Wishing you'd awaken in a hearse…

Being escorted to a place where you can finally
REST!
Not even giving AF if "rest" equals death.

Eternal darkness;
never having to wonder what's next.

Personally, I can't imagine that level of sadness.

The sounds of chains clinking in your memories.

This box doesn't come with silence??
Whyyy, can I STILL HEAR my thoughts??
I STILL hear him picking the locks on my door.

Squeezing my eyes tight doesn't help me
disappear anymore... I feel exposed.

Who ever knew you could run out of spaces to
bury your pain
Never knew I was insane, til now…
Who would've known it would bleed out?
Stitches popped!!
Bandage worn.
Just when I needed it to cover these thorns...
It fell completely off!
I wanted to be completely lost…

In my sadness, I stumbled upon the longitude
and latitude of my heart...
Only thing left is this microscopic part,
where you lived.
Didn't even have room for the kids.
So, they tend to miss out!!!
When you betray me, I scream, they shout.
I love harder, you drift...

It all began with a dark kiss.

A touch... A lisp...
Follow the breadcrumbs,
maybe you'll find what you've missed.

Make it Make sense

When past childhood traumas creep up on your
adult life,
Sometimes you can't think right.
In black communities we normalize,
We gas light, we fist fight, we stereotype…
our own damn selves.
This shit ain't our birthright!!
Quick, Alexa! Mapquest me out of this hell!!
I done sat with it, felt it, processed it, buried it,
resurrected it... buried it again!!
Even realized I tried to run from it in almost
every relationship I've been in!!
I meditated. I prayed!!
When dark knights came my way,
I slayed!!
Now MS cuttin' up, got me in this chair…

They talkn' bout I make it look easy!!
Like nah, when I least expect it, I hop in my
mind and my memories deceive me…
leading me to places I thought I'd left behind.
Mental shrines tend to be hard to release,
especially when history repeats
Somebody make it make sense.
This shit can't possibly be legit.

Stick Beside Me

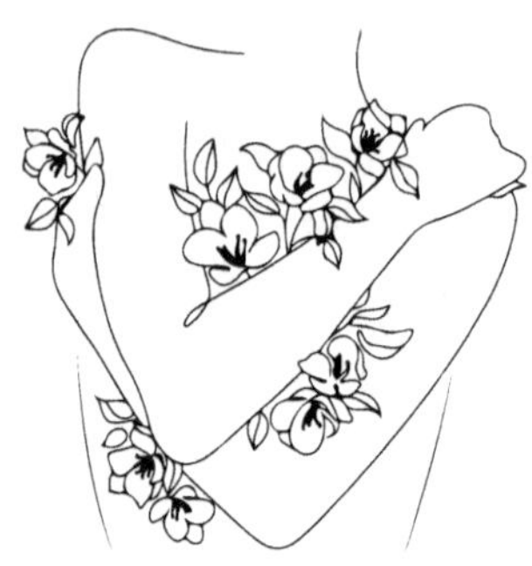

Someone said write yourself a love letter…
I'm thinking, where do I begin?
Lately I've been feeling like my very own
"homie, lover, friend."
Nobody fukkn with me like I'm rockn with me…
one thing bout NOW,
I'm gon' ALWAYS stick beside ME!
I'mma ride, I let that old gullible bitch die...
Wait, let me embrace that.
I was who I NEEDED to be to survive.
At one point on some people pleasing shit,
then I rised...
Ctrl - Alt - DELETED

Goal is to NEVER. AGAIN. Repeat it.

Lesson learned.
Chain broken.
No love lost.

Now on my Pac shit..
Like......picture me ROLLIN!

I flow, I glow, I grow.
Seeds planted;
patiently awaiting my breakthrough,
for what I've manifested to slide through.

Renewed health, stability.
Peace, mentally.

The ability to travel again.
To walk without assistive devices.
Props to me for learning to cope without vices!!
I fukkn love you Queen!!
You're a Goddess for real!!
An alchemist.
Your light beams!
NEVER underestimate what you're capable of!!
Manifestations finna be bustn' out the seams!!
Wealth, top tier health, and a life BEYOND your
WILDEST DREAMS!!!
You're moving w/ devine alignment, just wait
and see...
Swear this same scenery, bullshit been killing
me!!

Courage

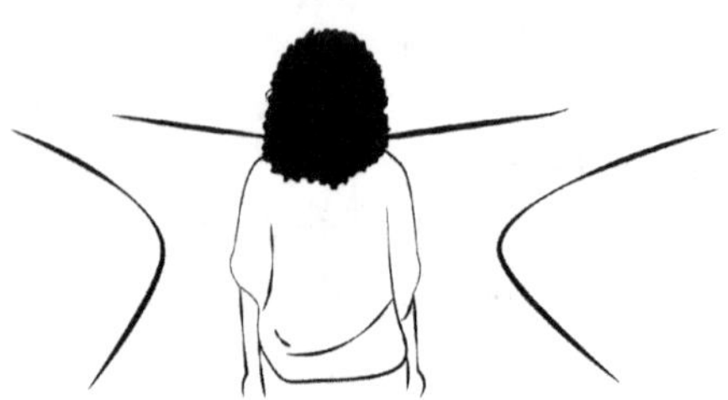

If everyone's so "unbothered"
Who's the worrisome one striving toward
change?
Who's the goal oriented dreamster, fighting
obstacles to build their name…
attempting to ignore fears; no longer letting
YEARS of procrastination hold them back?
Articulating with confidence, though courage is
what they lack.

Refused to Grow

We're not a family
We're just a group of humans posing as one
Avoiding being done
Placing band aids over wounds and calling it
"fun."
Human, being fake.
Unable to relate.
Outgrown each other,
been so long with each other it's like breathing.
However, each breath could be deceiving.
It's what you don't see that can be toxic.

It's what we didn't speak on, that robbed it…
 - US of our true glow.
You pretended to be happy, yet refused to know.
- Refused to grow.

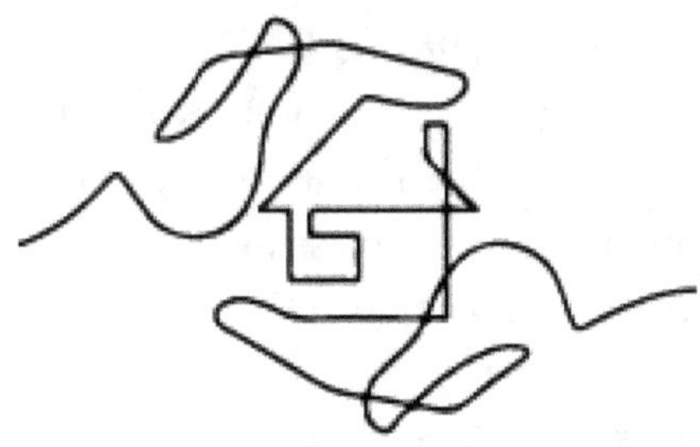

High Key Lies

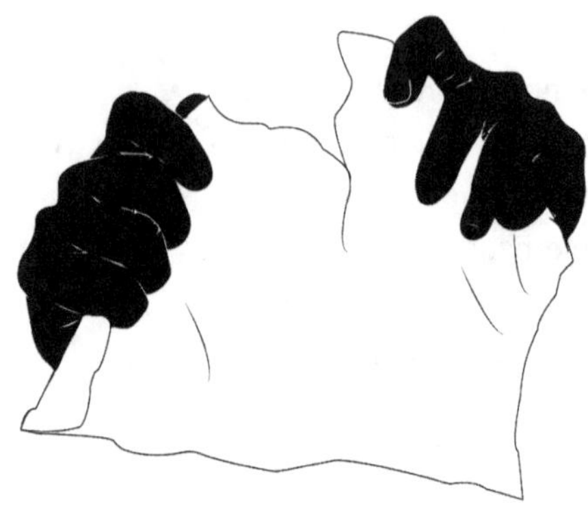

How bout I was today years old;
FORTY, when I realized my mom's STILL
technically never accepted my reality.
Like, I'm gay azFUCK!!!
But in her presence, only gay "respectfully."
Yet negligently, she's STILL been low-key
judging my sexuality.

I've been living a lie!!???
Whole life lived on HIGH-KEY LIES
Clearly I've been delusional to believe I'd ever
fully receive, her blessing
As a teen, homeless a FEW times,
and when I needed to return home—
She kept me guessing.
Blamed it on HIM.

Now all these years later, therapy revealed it was
NEVER 'cause of "him".
It was HER judgment.
HER;
STILL feeling like my lifestyle was a sin...
But I needed you.
Why I always gotta cry… kick, scream
Then silence my pain;
bury it and pretend shit ain't what it seems!!?

Whole time probably burying the pain in
somebody's daughter!!
All cause of being denied of Mommy's brick and
mortar
I gotta digress...
Not quite ready to unpack this foolishness.
*Takes deep breath

It's ALL Love

Idky, I have a thing
For light skinned queens,
I just do.
But don't get it twisted
Cuz I gotta eye for butter pecan 'ricans
And a sweet tooth for chocolate drops too.
(Maybe it's the artist in me)
Standing on bus stops
Suckn' on lollipops…
Was gay all my life,
young mind couldn't admit it.
Mama judged, so I hid it…
But when "bestie" came through, I HIT IT!
Now I'm grown;
screaming FukK y'all's opinions!!
Fuk is the difference!?
I like what I love…
I just prefer to meticulously lay pipe, while
others chase behind slugs…
It's all love!!

Dissolve

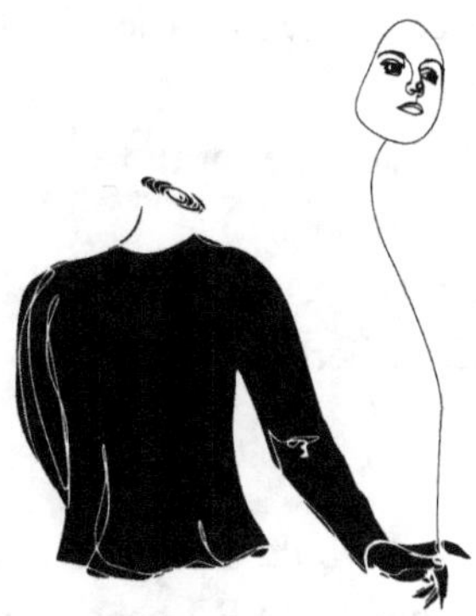

I've been loving you forever. PRIORITIZING
you forever.
Ask me if I've ever been prioritized?
The answer is NEVER.
There was always a reason, an excuse,
accompanied by mental and emotional abuse...
Manipulation.
All my life I've been waiting
But now I'm mf tied, been beyond tired..

Every time you promised things would get
better, you lied
Even family therapy was a lost cause
You said your worst fear was losing me forever,
but…

Anyways...I remember when my pops used to
take me on summer vacations.

I made sure I'd always get a postcard to mail
back home to you.
Figured you could live vicariously through my
postal imagery
You never thanked me for those.
It didn't matter though,
I'd still send them year after year, from every
city, no matter where we'd go.

I'm 40 now…
who'd think shit would be worse!?
Who'd think that AFTER I became progressed in
this MS disability shit, you'd STILL find a way
to twist the knife
As if I wasn't already hurt!!!

At this point I feel ashamed to speak on my
experiences
Embarrassed,
Nervous to speak out on how I feel,
Out of fear that you'd absorb my hurt then
project it
More gas lighting, narcissistically injuring me
more, mentally.

This shit hurts so bad I can't even think of the
words to poetically confide in the pages of my
journal freely.
I just want to be done.

I just wanna be me.
Authentically.
But how?? You're my mom...
I love you beyond words, but how???
How do you let go??
When all you ever wanted is to be seen by the
person who gave you life and watched you grow

How can I just move forward and ignore the
pain...
How, how do I move forward and just dissolve
everything?

I Am NOT Your Alter

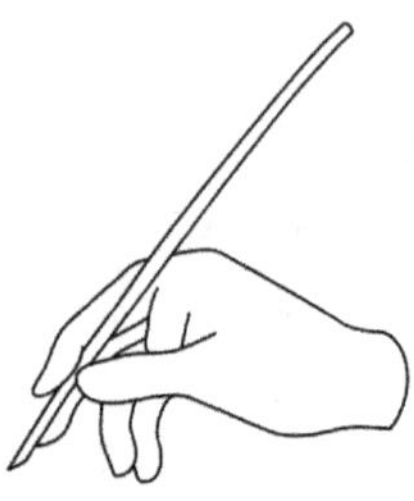

I am not your alter.
You cannot kneel and confess your burdens.
You cannot prey, yes PREY upon me.
I am not your deity,
sent to absolve, heal, and transmute.
This work is for YOU.
I've learned that I am MY priority.
I am MY God.
My healer.
MY shadow boxer when shit gets bleak.
I am not a light filled place to plant your seeds.
This nourishment is now reserved for ME!
I've learned my lessons.
I take back my power;
opening my doors for blessings.

Sumthn' Slight

I tell these ladies..
Miss me with the bullshit.
Cause I aim for hearts.
Don't come at me with elementary beef…
'Cause I keep a loaded clip of thoughts…
I'll lyrically dismantle your mental;
…have you weeping in the dark.
Eloquently convey your issue...
Or I'll teach you how to talk!

Moral of the story:
Don't start shit you can't POSSIBLY finish;
with an individual like a lyrical chemist.
...and I would call you a "BITCH";
but, clearly I'm different.

Melanin

And you ask..
What that melanin be like??
I say, it CAN be that free life
That prana filled, INNER G life
If u SEE right

Activate that third eye, then you'll see light.

You see, that hennessey smooth like melanated skin.

Yet toxic,
like white lies we've been programmed to let in…
and I… ain't tryna knock ya shit
Just get you to realize that,
the blood running through your veins is similar to liquid computer chips,

If used right, it joins you at the hip with
ancestors.
Once explored,
you'd innerstand the weapon to use against
Rothschilds & Rockefellers…
and I ain't talkin' bout Hov
But you CAN change clothes;
Break the mold.

Overstand, the melanin is more than pigment
and worth more than gold
Do your research; we possess the mother gene,
ever wonder why our organs are being
trafficked, and sold??
Negus bodies poppn' up gutted,
before a tag hits the toe…

Get connected,
well respected;
by self FIRST.
Then, spark flames in another, before your
picture's on a shirt
Body rollin' in a hearse…
With no story left behind.

When asked, what that melanin be like!?
I said, like astrophysics… similar to the sky,
only with no limits!

Cleaning out my closet

How do I get the pain out??
I've been learning to master alchemy,
but sometimes my brain hits reroute.

Taking me back to vices,
all I know is I don't like it.

How my father die,
MS relapse land me in a wheelchair,
and you STILL refuse to try!?

You still avoid accountability.
Love STILL DENIED.

All I wanted was sympathy,
empathy maybe…

Instead,
I get MORE trauma;
and to think,
I'm receiving this from YOU..
My OWN got damn mama!

They say that I should just accept you for who
you are.
But how can I do that,
when all you keep leaving me with is scars.

Scars from YOUR childhood,
scars from YOUR past

Scars you never healed,
and thought they wouldn't last…
But they do!

And the same hurt you're causing ME,
is part of what they caused you

This curse has to end.

You talk to me like I'm your friend,
when all I wanted was someone to believe in…

To seek comfort, safety and emotional support

But when shit gets rough, all you do is abort

Age 40 and you STILL don't know how to love
me… but how can I be mad at you?

You can't give me something you never knew

So what I'll strive to do,
is make sure that the people that I love,
will never look at me,
the way I look at you.

SEEDLESS SOIL

When I say I'm blessed
I'm not only referring to money or material
things
I'm referring to situations that were sent to
destroy my soul.
They touched my spirit instead.

Dark night of the soul made me WHOLE again
Replenished my soul
Growth was always the goal
But somehow I became distracted…
Hijacked, spiritually redacted.
A genetically modified vessel…

They thought removing the seeds from my fruit
would dim my light
Whole time it intensified my focus by increasing
my sight
Like, what are you all trying to hide from me??
It has to be some level of POWER that only a
CLEAN undistracted mind can see…
Now it's calling me!

Greetings from the rabbit hole!
They didn't know I was a Blue Ray Starseed
They didn't realize that my connection with
source was the most vital resource that they
could never
retrieve
EYE SEE what they want.

But these roots don't falter; they know
EXACTLY where to go
How to grow…
They've traveled this road lifetimes before I
existed in this physical world
I simply hit the portal and became the new
digital girl sent to wreak havoc in this matrix
Fukk up, figure shit out…
Stumble, trip, dislocate hips…
Be abandoned in the dark.
Be left alone in parks.
To explore…

To have the world shut its door on me.
Thankfully the light was always attracted to the
darkness in me.

Turns out the tunnel was the illusion.
The light within me remained lit…
My need to know,
My will to evolve and grow overpowered any
low vibrational nonsense.

You see, sometimes our weakest moments can
be alchemized into our biggest strengths
Massive gifts; in disguise…
My pops always said I was an angel in HIS eyes.
That my inquisitive ways made me "special, not
annoying."
That he'd never understood where I'd get my
questions from
But that he "always thought they were good."
Said he'd never seen anything like it, "especially
in a child, your age."
But that I'd "always been this way."

So in my eyes, I was divinely designed to crack
codes in a system that was created to
intentionally
deceive my mind and lead me astray.

I keep asking to "manifest a life BEYOND my
wildest dreams."
Whole time, I AM IT!! I AM my ancestor's
WILDEST dream
As the kundalini continued to coil,
I realized, I am an incarnation sent to PUSH
THROUGH SEEDLESS SOIL

Star Seed

While people are in awe of me, I'm in awe of
them being in awe of me.
Sometimes I even get stuck,
Searching for the right words to say at the right
time...
When I'm at my highest, or my lowest…
Hear my soul speak.

Note to YOU, Turned Note to Cell'f

I'm so used to you not loving me anymore;
I can't always take you serious now,
When you try to…

If you aren't CONSISTENTLY loving on you,
How do you expect anyone to love on me?
Prioritize cell'f FIRST
Learn to embrace flaws and love ME;
unconditionally.

Love w/o Conditions

Who am I to ask of your love?
When you're barely hanging on...
How selfish of me.
How inconsiderate,
When you're drowning in your fears and
practicality begging to be free
We conversed about the universe,
Set flames to sunsets,

Floated on waves across coastal plains and
chased down comets in Kemet.
The way our love was set up,
I would've never known you weren't in it.
Mentally taken beyond previous limits,
Fukk Bennet!
I'm all up in it...
Sign sealed deliverance.
Now pondering words like, finished.
And I thought we'd just got started

LIVING was what we always wanted,
Existing was far too minuscule.
All I thought I needed was you.
But I had to let go,
Watch you drift off into those sunsets alone.
Watch you vandalize that place we once called
home…
Unbeknownst to me,
Your journey was attached to comfort zones.
Now solo, learning to live without conditions,
Beaming light and it's splendid!!
Beautiful, radiant...
How quickly the tables spent…

New Boundaries, Who Dis?

As you can see, this time isn't like those before.
Having a hard time reopening my heart's door…

Now that you SAY you've torn down your
wall...
It seems as if I've built up some bricks of my
own.
They serve as protection,
For the area of my heart that you still reside in.
No longer worthy of being called a friend,
I greet you with a regretful hello.

NO Dump zone!

You THINK you can mentally mistreat me when
you feel lost and defeated
When you're not sure how to approach life,
Or just CHOOSE not to realistically receive it.
You will NOT emotionally dump on me!!
You will not place blame on ME for issues YOU
created, then mentally abated cause you felt
you couldn't deal.
This emotional ferris wheel ain't shit to play
with,
Don't come fukkn up my day with things
consistency could handle.
I'll say this, then Ill digress.
Every fukkn body's got problems!!
Stop lying and concealing yours…
That won't wash them away.
They'll just overflow and drown you behind
closed doors!!
Tear down that bullshit ass wall!!
Bricks are missing anyway...
The toxicity you're concealing is leaking out day
by day.
Guilt brings pain, storms bring rain...
Darkness facilitates light..
You get where I'm going right!!?
Don't think I'm finna' hide with you

How 'bout you face this world with TRUTH!
Be honest with yourself FIRST!
Know that there's people who have it way
worse.
You're a good person; but you're not innocent
Stop portraying yourself as perfect and you
won't be let down
Learn to be vulnerable, fukk who's standing
'round!!!

No Poet

I ain't no poet,
I just talk a lot…
I ain't no genius,
I just think a lot...
And read a lot...
Don't ignore what I see a lot...
I used to smoke weed a lot;
Then learned it's more to life than pot.

Good Vibe

I plan to build up this space. For me!
I think I'll call it the good vibe bubble..lol corny
right?
But trust, they'll be NOTHING cheesy about
this space.
With pure energy, and infinite high vibrations
I'll keep it laced!!
No traces of fear,
Zero darkness resides here…
Unless I choose to invite the moon in;
to replenish my peace and demolish thy sin
Rejuvenate inner power and facilitate zen.
In this place I'll attempt to not fight; nor engage
myself in unnecessary plights.
I'll continue to heal here.
Hope shit never gets REAL here!!
'Cause although I'm trying to be better, that
hood nigga is still here!!
I will always be a work in progress.
I feel how I dress… catch me on the right day,
and you'll get wronged.
Unless you catch me with my good vibe bubble
on!!

Twin

You were my ladybug
A firefly in my nights full of mosquitoes
You flew in out of nowhere,
Divinely timed;
Shook my mind, shimmied down my spine,
and...
Let's just say I ain't been the same since!!!

Ascension

Don't get it twisted I stay lifted
Honestly I'm gifted,
Galactic dust I'm filled with.
Blue Ray Star Seed
Reacquainting myself with alchemy
Frequently raising frequencies
Transmuting darkness into light
Learning to surrender to resistance
No need for fight or flight.
The messenger,
Now learning to listen.
Transition.
Grow.

Unlearning self-imposed conditions on self-love,
Based on what others tend to show…

Like a butterfly blossoming from its cocoon,
I may make mistakes…

But with grace,
I'll stay lifted
Continuously ascending toward the moon…

Silver Lining

Drowned in my darkness,
Got lost in my mistakes;
and found forgiveness.

ABOUT THE AUTHOR

Renowned as the enigmatic wordsmith S.P.A.Z. (spreading. peace. awareness. zeal), Lateasha Owens journey into the world of artistic expression began in grade school. Creative writing became her sanctuary; she eloquently conveyed her emotions, seeking a voice amidst the pages.

Lateasha garnered acclaim, winning numerous poetry and creative writing contests. These victories culminated in a pivotal book deal that beckoned her towards literary greatness.

However, her fear of judgment held her words hostage. She never accepted the deal or submitted her poems for publishing.

Lateasha Owens narrative is one of resilience, transformation, and the triumphant emergence from the shadows. Her artistry not only graced the streets of Philadelphia but served as a testament to the indomitable spirit that perseveres against adversity.

In embracing the vulnerability of releasing her
book, Lateasha invites the world to bear witness
to her profound journey—a tale woven with
threads of pain, strength, and the unyielding
power of artistic expression.